ORIGAMI

FOR

BEGINNERS

THE CREATIVE WORLD OF PAPER FOLDING

FLORENCE TEMKO

TUTTLE Publishing

Tokyo | Rutland, Vermont | Singapore

Contents

Published by Tuttle Publishing, an imprint of
Periplus Editions (HK) Ltd.

www.tuttlepublishing.com

© 1991, 2002 Charles E. Tuttle Publishing Co.
All rights reserved.
LCC Card No. 2002103710

ISBN 978-0-8048-3313-4

Published in 1991
Second edition 2002

Printed in Singapore

Photography by Andy Wong
Styling and folds by Magdalene Ong, Grace Tay

17 16 15 14   13 12 11 10   1410CP

TUTTLE PUBLISHING® is a registered trademark of Tuttle Publishing, a division of Periplus Editions (HK) Ltd.

Introduction

Origami, the art of paper folding, is fun and easy! Even if you have never folded paper before, you'll find the objects in *Origami for Beginners* easy to make. As you flip through the pages of this book, you'll surely spot something that interests you. Even if it looks difficult, it's really not, so go ahead and give it a try. Let's say you find the Elephant especially appealing. If you follow the step-by-step directions carefully, you'll get good results. And when you fold the Elephant a second time, you'll discover that you can make it even better and faster than the first time.

Origami is believed to have originated in China, but the craft developed most fully in Japan. For centuries, Japanese origami was closely associated with traditional ceremonies, but over time the craft became a popular family pastime. In recent years, origami has spread all over the world to such an extent that origami clubs have sprung up in many countries. Through these clubs, origami enthusiasts meet regularly, hold exhibitions, and disseminate information through newsletters and other publications.

While origami is an ideal activity for children, many adults have also discovered that paper folding is a creative, challenging, and relaxing hobby. Some paper folders have created designs that are widely recognized as valuable works of art.

Like any other craft, origami is based on a few fundamental techniques. Before you begin folding, be sure to look over the next section, "Practical Information", so that you're familiar with these simple yet important origami guidelines.

Practical Information

Symbols
The folding symbols in this book conform to a system used by paper folders throughout the world. For the most part, the symbols are self-explanatory and can usually be followed even without referring to the written instruction.

Fold in this direction.

Fold along this line.

- - - - - - - - - - - - - - -

Existing crease.

———————————

Valley fold: Fold toward you to create a valley.

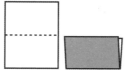

Mountain fold: Fold away from you to the back; this creates a mountain. (Always check whether you're making a valley fold or a mountain fold.)

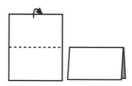

Fold under another flap.

Illustration has been enlarged.

Turn back to front, i.e., turn origami over.

Model
One completed origami figure.

Base
Basic starting point for making different models. Three bases are shown in this book: Blintz Base, Kite Base, and Diamond Base.

Paper
Most of the models in this book are made from square pieces of paper with widths of between 6" and 10" (15 and 25 centimeters). If a special size or kind of paper is needed for a particular model, this is clearly specified. Prepackaged origami paper, which is usually colored on one side and white on the other side, is handy to use. Unless specified otherwise, the directions in this book are for paper that is colored on one side only. You can, however, experiment using other types of papers. All crisp, fairly thin papers such as gift wrap, or bond, computer, and stationery papers are suitable for origami. When you cut paper to a desired size, be sure that you cut it into exact squares or rectangles. Some projects look better when folded with double-sided origami paper—either special origami paper that has different colors on the front and the back, or ordinary paper, like stationery, that happens to be colored on both sides. You can also make your own double-sided paper by pasting together different papers, and then cutting them to the desired dimensions.

DIAMOND BASE (Use any square)

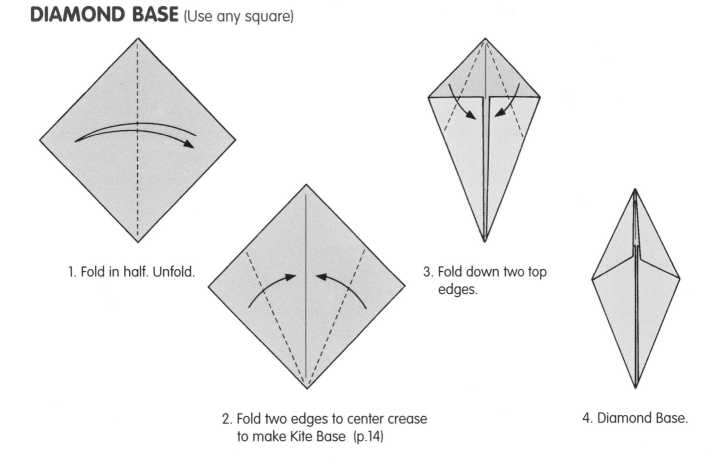

1. Fold in half. Unfold.

2. Fold two edges to center crease to make Kite Base (p.14)

3. Fold down two top edges.

4. Diamond Base.

SQUAWKER TOY (Use any square)

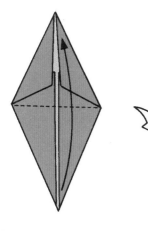

1. Fold a Diamond Base. Fold up lower half.

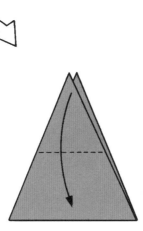

2. Fold down front flap only.

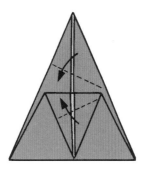

3. From right side, fold two flaps so that their edges meet along horizontal middle division.

4. Unfold last step.

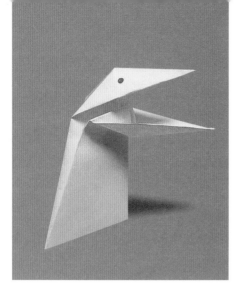

Party Favors

From 10" squares, make one Squawker Toy for each place setting. Both young and old will be delighted with these adorable birds. Use bright colors to fold the Squawker Toys and staple strips of colored paper to both sides of their backs to create fancy tails.

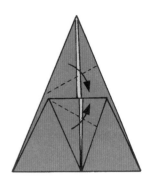

5. From left side, fold two flaps so that their edges meet along horizontal middle division.

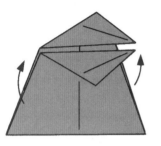

6. Mountain fold bottom half of paper in half. Let Squawker's beak settle naturally into creases made in Steps 3 and 5.

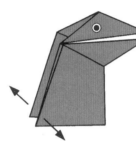

7. Squawker Toy. Pull sides apart to make beak open.

SHARK (Use any square)

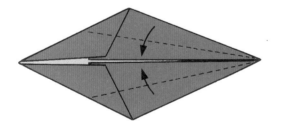

1. Fold a Diamond Base. Fold edges in.

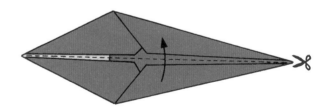

2. Make small cut at long, narrow end. Fold in half.

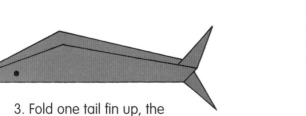

3. Fold one tail fin up, the other down. Shark.

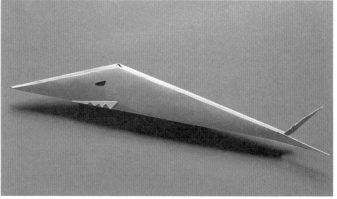

Pirate's Hat, Pilgrim's Bonnet, Robot, Tropical Fish

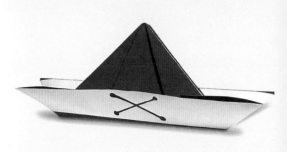

PIRATE'S HAT (Use any square)

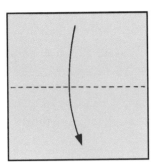

1. Fold in half.

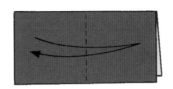

2. Fold in half. Unfold.

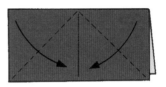

3. Fold corners down.

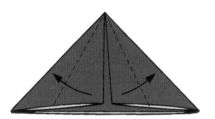

4. Flip flaps out.

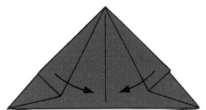

5. Unfold.

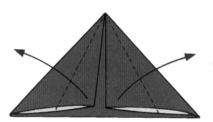

6. Poke finger into bottom opening of left flap. Swing flap up and, following creases, flatten. Repeat with right flap.

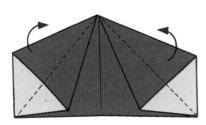

7. Mountain fold to back.

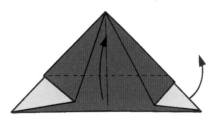

8. Fold up front flap as far as possible. Repeat on back.

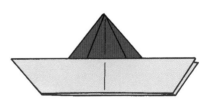

9. Pirate's Hat.

Wearable Hats

Use a 23" square for an adult's hat or an 18" square for a child's hat. Fold with newspaper, gift wrap, wallpaper, or construction paper. Decorate the finished hat with feathers, paper cutouts, and stickers. Attach string or elastic to make a chin strap.

Squash Fold

Steps 4 through 6 of the Pirate's Hat make up a common folding technique called a "squash fold". As the name implies, the paper, guided by crease, is squashed into the desired fold.

PILGRIM'S BONNET (Use any square)

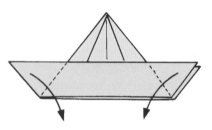

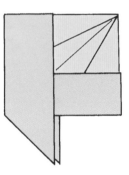

1. Fold a Pirate's Hat. Fold front pointed flaps down.

2. Grasp front and pull out slightly to the right. At the same time, grasp back and pull slightly backwards to the left. Flatten.

3. Pilgrim's Bonnet.

ROBOT (Use any square)

TROPICAL FISH
(Use any square)

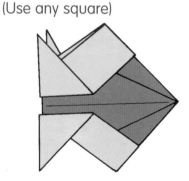

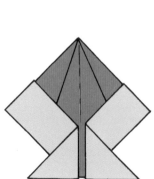

1. Make a Pilgrim's Bonnet. Separate two front flaps by folding top flap back.

2. Robot.

For a Tropical Fish, make a Robot and turn it sideways.

Aquarium

Tropical Fish and Sharks (p. 6) may not always be friends in nature, but they can be in an aquarium. Try inventing other kinds of origami fish by varying the folds, and experiment using leaf designs to make water plants.

Skyscraper

SKYSCRAPER (Use a 3" x 11" strip of paper)

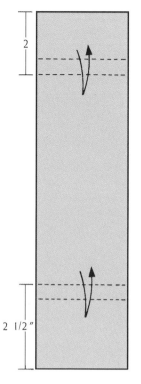

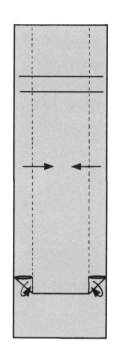

1. Make pleats by folding mountain and valley folds; i.e. fold flaps down, then back up.

2. Unfold two top creases.

3. Fold up two small corners.

4. Open two small corners and squash flat while folding side edges in. Two triangles should form at base of tower. Don't fold lower part of paper.

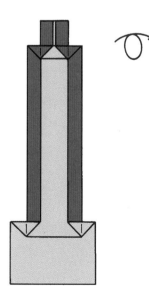

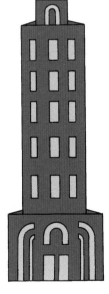

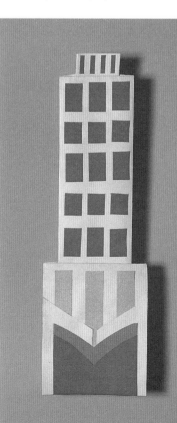

5. Once more, pleat top creases. Repeat Steps 3 and 4 with two small corners near the top.

6. Turn back to front.

7. Skyscraper.

Christmas Star, Star Earrings, Gift Wrap Decoration

CHRISTMAS STAR (Use a 4" square of double-sided paper or foil gift wrap)

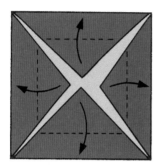

1. Fold a Blintz Base (p. 12). Fold all corners to outside edges.

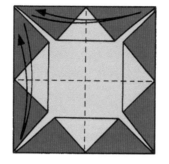

2. Fold in quarters. Unfold. Turn back to front.

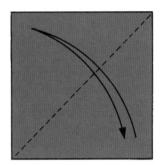

3. Diagonally fold in half. Unfold.

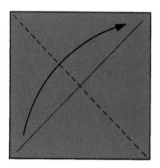

4. Diagonally fold in half again. Leave folded.

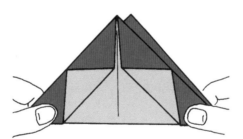

5. Grasp opposite corners. Push into a star shape.

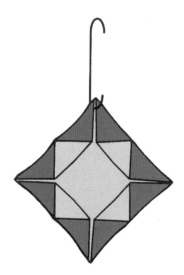

6. Christmas Star. Attach an ornament hook.

STAR EARRINGS
(Use two 2" squares)

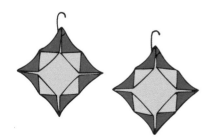

Fold two Christmas Stars. Attach earring fittings.

GIFT WRAP DECORATION

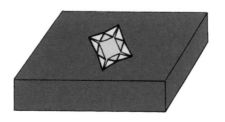

Apply glue to the edges of the back of a Christmas Star and place on a package.

Blintz Base, Quicky Gift Envelope, Layered Card, Last-minute Greeting Card

BLINTZ BASE (Use any square)

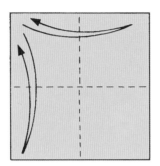

1. Fold in quarter. Unfold.

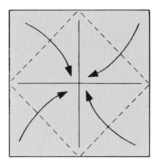

2. Fold corners in.

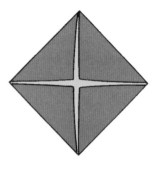

3. Blintz Base.

QUICKY GIFT ENVELOPE (Use a 10"or larger square of gift wrap)

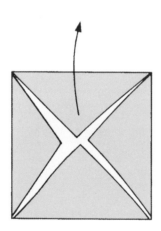

1. Fold a Blintz Base. Open one flap.

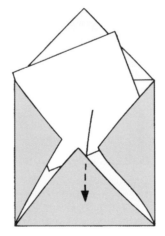

2. Insert a card, a scarf, stamps, money, or other flat gift.

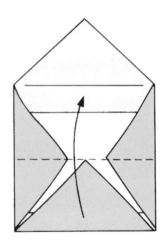

3. Fold bottom edge up.

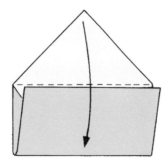

4. Fold down flap.

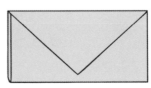

5. Quicky Gift Envelope.

The Blintz Base

The Blintz Base is named after a pastry that is made by taking a square of dough and folding its four corners to the center. Using this easy Blintz Base as a starting point, you can fold many different models, several of which are shown here.

LAYERED CARD (Use three squares: 4", 5", and 6")

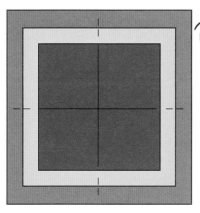

1. Fold each square in quarters. Unfold. Center squares and glue, one on top of the other. Turn back to front so that largest square faces up.

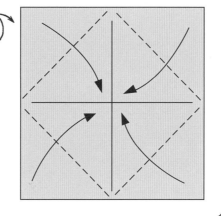

2. Fold corners to middle.

Back

Front

3. Layered card.

LAST-MINUTE GREETING CARD (Use a square of gift wrap)

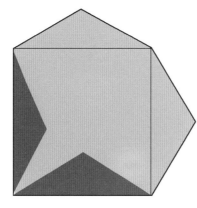

1. Fold a Bintz Base. Open flaps and write greeting inside. Close flaps.

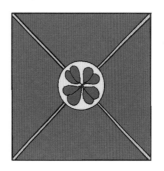

2. Add a sticker to seal the card.

Kite Base, Pine Tree, Trick Mouse, Fantastic Flyer Airplane

KITE BASE (Use any square)

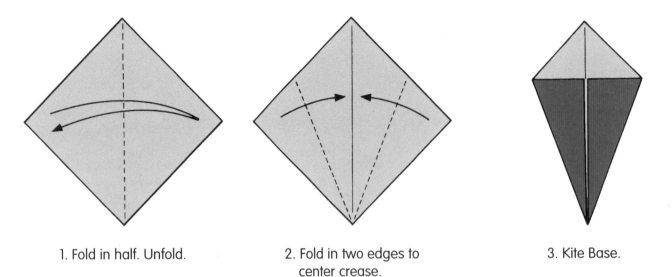

1. Fold in half. Unfold.

2. Fold in two edges to center crease.

3. Kite Base.

PINE TREE (Use a green square)

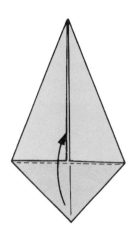

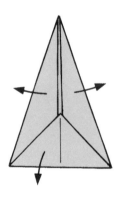

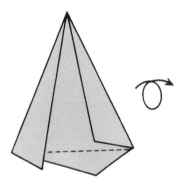

1. Fold a Kite Base. Place as shown. Fold up triangular flap.

2. Loosen all three flaps.

3. Turn back to front and place tree upright.

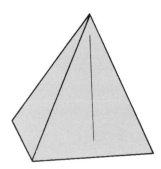

4. Pine Tree.

For a unique Christmas card, flatten Pine Tree and send with a note explaining how it can stand upright.

TRICK MOUSE (Use a 2" square)

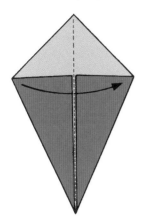

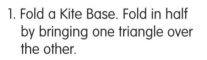

1. Fold a Kite Base. Fold in half by bringing one triangle over the other.

2. Trick Mouse. Tap tail to make mouse jump.

For better action, make very sharp creases. Gluing the bottom two triangular flaps together will also help.

FANTASTIC FLYER AIRPLANE (Use any square and a paper clip)

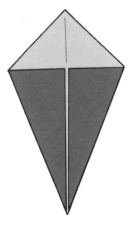

1. Fold a Kite Base. Turn back to front.

2. Fold edges in.

3. Mountain fold in half (refer to "Practical information", p. 3).

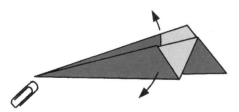

4. Place wings at 90° to the body. Attach a paper clip to the nose.

5. Fantastic Flyer Airplane. Throw airplane upward.

Gift Box, Covered Box, Easter Basket

GIFT BOX (Use any square)

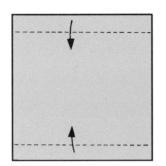

1. Place colored side up. Fold in two edges of equal widths.

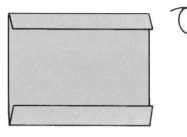

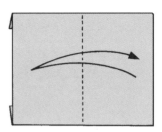

2. Turn back to front.

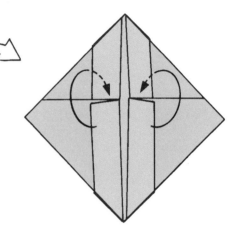

3. Fold in half. Unfold

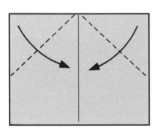

4. Fold corners in.

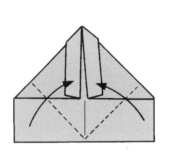

5. Fold corners in.

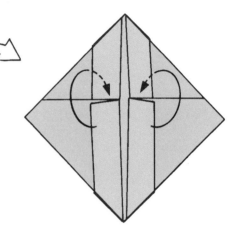

6. Tuck bottom cuffs into top cuffs.

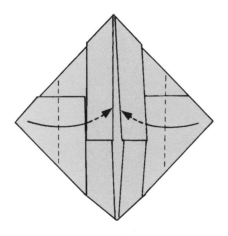

7. Fold corners under cuffs.

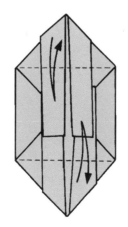

8. Fold top and bottom corners in. Unfold.

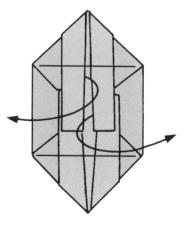

9. Open box by lifting up cuffs.

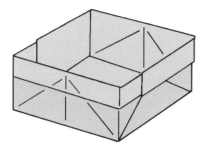

10. Sharply crease corners at 90° angles. Gift Box.

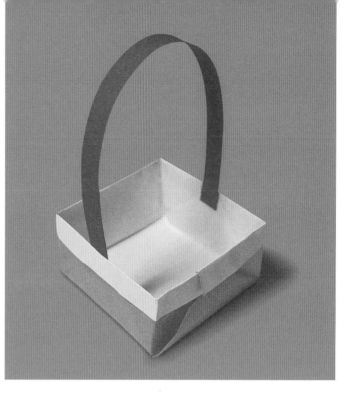

COVERED BOX (Use two squares)

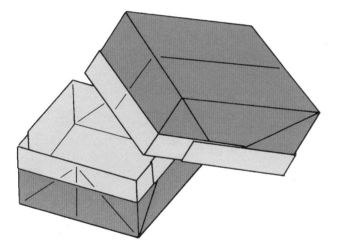

Fold two Gift Boxes, one from a square about 1/2" smaller than the other. The larger box will serve as a lid for the smaller box.

EASTER BASKET (Use a square and a strip of paper)

Fold a Gift Box. Cut a strip of paper and fold it lengthwise in half for a handle. Staple or tuck the ends under the cuffs of the box. Strengthen the basket by cutting a piece of cardboard the same size as the bottom of the box and placing it inside.

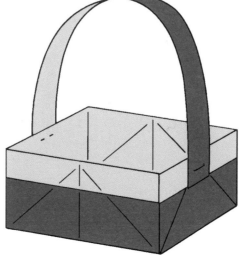

Earrings, Icicles, Sunburst

EARRINGS (Use two 2" squares)

1. Make two airplanes (p. 15).

2. Attach earring fittings.

ICICLES (Use 4" squares of foil gift wrap)

1. Fold airplanes (p. 15.)

2. Icicles. Attach ornament and hang icicles on a Christmas tree.

SUNBURST (Use large, bright yellow squares)

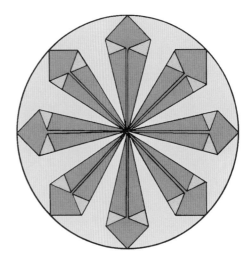

1. Fold eight Airplanes (p. 15), stopping at Step 3.

2. Glue in a circle on a posterboard. Sunburst.

Cat, Standing Cat, Cat Family

HEAD (Use any square)

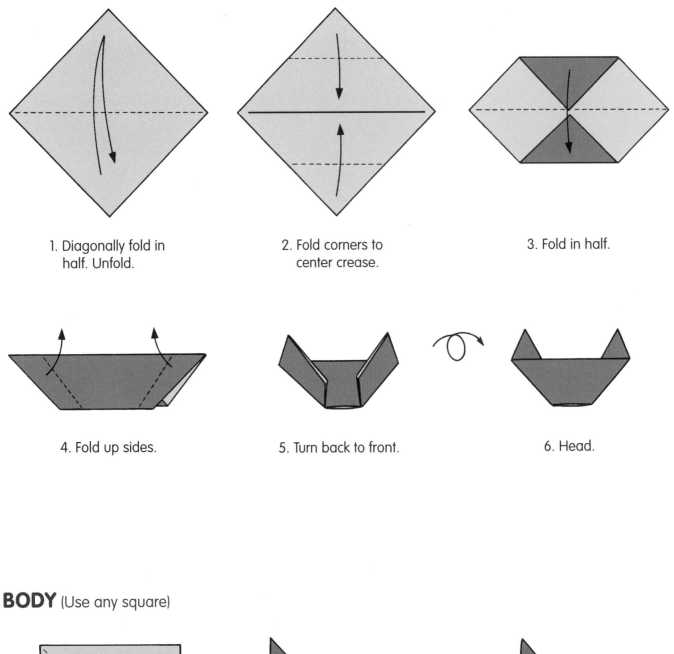

1. Diagonally fold in half. Unfold.

2. Fold corners to center crease.

3. Fold in half.

4. Fold up sides.

5. Turn back to front.

6. Head.

BODY (Use any square)

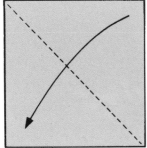

1. Diagonally fold in half.

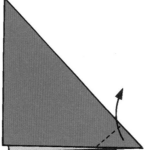

2. Fold up to make tail.

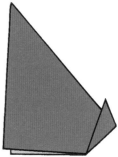

3. Body.

Cards and notepapers

Cat lovers everywhere will enjoy receiving gifts, letters, invitations, and holiday cards decorated with these origami cats. You might want to experiment using different types of colored and patterned paper, and drawing in the eyes, nose and whiskers with a felt tip pen.

ASSEMBLY

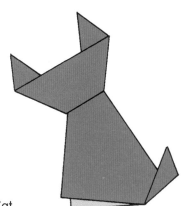

1. Insert top corner of Body in pocket of head.

2. Cat.

STANDING CAT (Use any square)

The Cat stands up if you unfold the tail. Open the whole body, and wrap the tail around the front and back while closing the body. This procedure is called an "outside reverse fold".

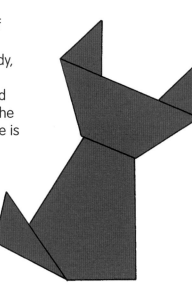

CAT FAMILY (Use 4", 6", and 8" squares)

To make kittens, use two 4" squares. Then make the adult cats using 8" squares for the bodies and 6" squares for the head.

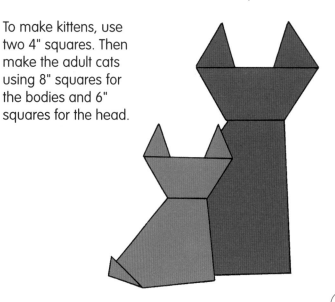

Space Rocket, Napkin Ring or Photo Holder, Car

SPACE ROCKET (Use about a 3" x 11" strip of paper)

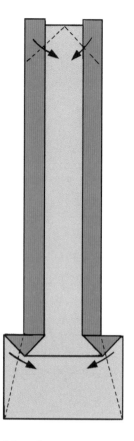

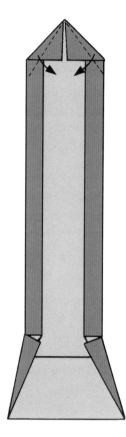

1. Fold a Skyscraper (p. 9) but make only the bottom pleat. Fold corners in at both top and bottom.

2. Fold top corners in. Turn back to front.

3. Space Rocket.

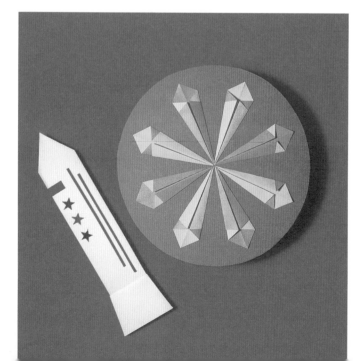

NAPKIN RING OR PHOTO

HOLDER (Use about a 3" x 11" strip of paper)

Fold a Skyscraper (p. 9) but make only the bottom pleat. Bend into a circle and glue or tape together in a place that cannot be seen. For a Napkin Ring that also serves as a place card, write a name on the square front. To use as a Photo Holder, simply fix a photo to the front.

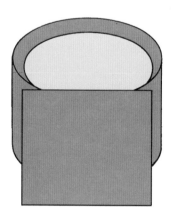

The Car

The Car shown below can be made, with minor changes, into many types of cars—family cars, racing cars, even antique cars. The directions here show how to make a car using a square, but you can make a longer, sleeker model if you use a rectangle.

CAR (Use any square)

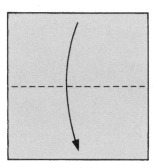

1. Fold in half.

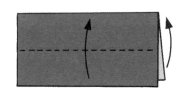

2. Fold front flap up. Fold back flap up.

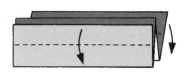

3. Fold front flap down. Fold back flap down.

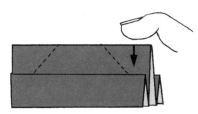

4. As shown, push top center fold down between side folds until corner extends below bottom. This makes a wheel. Repeat at the opposite end to make the other wheel.

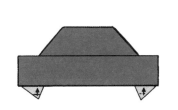

5. Fold up bottom corners of wheels. Turn back to front.

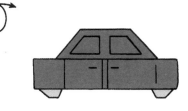

6. Car.

BOAT (Use any square)

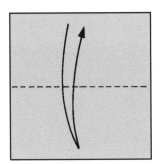

1. Fold in half. Unfold.

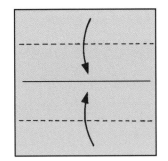

2. Fold edges in.

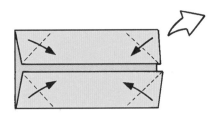

3. Fold four corners in.

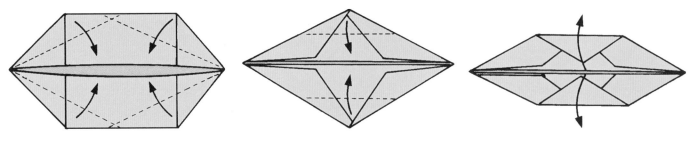

4. Fold four corners to middle.

5. Fold corners to middle.

6. Reach in deep and spread sides apart.

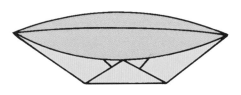

7. Boat. Make a stronger model by returning to Step 1 and starting with the colored side up. Proceed to Step 7.

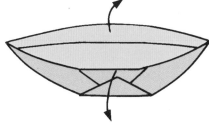

8. Pull top edges to the outside while pushing up bottom of boat, turning it inside out.

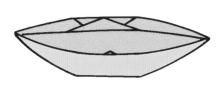

9. Inside-out Boat.

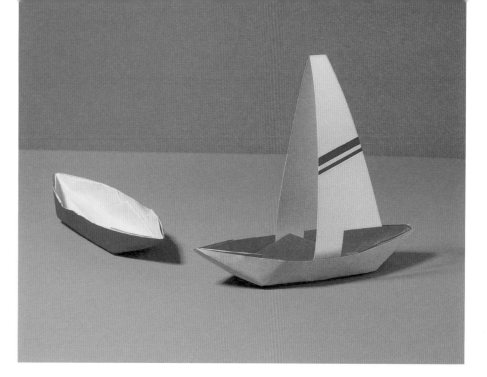

Bathtub Frolic

These paper boats float, but they last longer if they are made from waxed paper. To strengthen them even more, staple their sides.

SAILBOAT BASKET (Use an 8" square and a 2" x 10" rectangle)

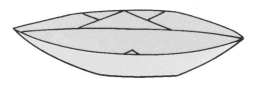

1. Make a Boat from the square.

2. Fold rectangle in half.

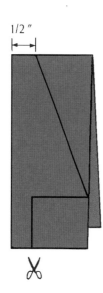

1/2"

3. Cut out a sail. Leave 1/2" of folded edge remaining at top of sail.

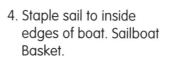

4. Staple sail to inside edges of boat. Sailboat Basket.

Elephant

HEAD (Use any square)

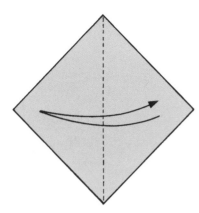

1. Fold. Unfold.

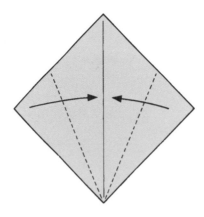

2. Fold edges in to center crease. (This makes a Kite Base.)

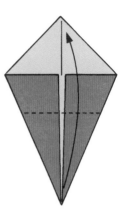

3. Fold up.

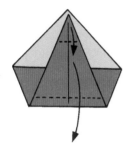

4. Fold tip down. Fold down again to form a pleat.

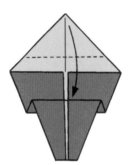

5. Fold top corner to the pleat.

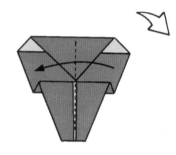

6. Fold in half.

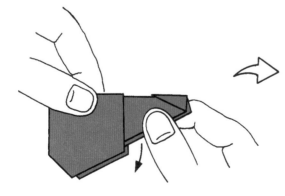

7. Pull down trunk. Make trunk stay in place by pressing area around the ear.

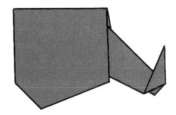

8. Pull away tip of trunk and press in place. Head.

Shaping

To make the head rounder in shape, try mountain folding all the corners. Or instead of making mountain folds at the top corners of the head, you can make "reverse folds"—folds formed by pushing the corners in between the two layers of paper.

Mammonth Elephant

Fold an Elephant from 36" or larger squares of construction paper. Reinforce finished model by gluing pieces of cardboard in places where they cannot be seen.

Jewelry

Make small Elephants, gluing the bodies and heads together. Laminate with coatings of white glue and use as earrings and brooches.

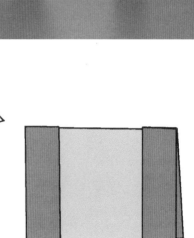

BODY (Use any square)

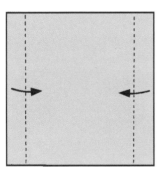

1. Fold in two edges.   2. Mountain fold in half.   3. Body.

ASSEMBLY

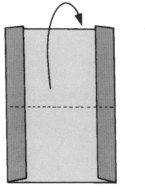

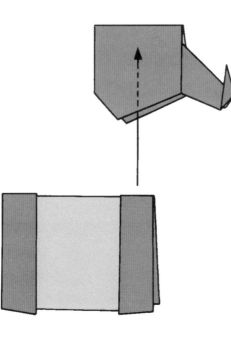

1. Open both body and head slightly. Slide body into pleat behind the trunk.

2. Elephant.

Furniture Units 1
BASIC UNIT, CHAIR, SIDE TABLE OR FOOTSTOOL

BASIC UNIT (Use two 6" x 4" rectangles)

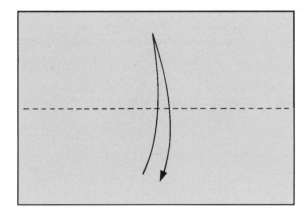

1. Fold first rectangle in half. Unfold.

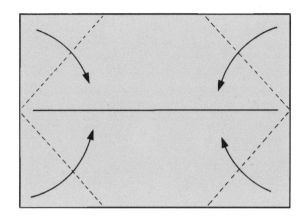

2. Fold in all corners.

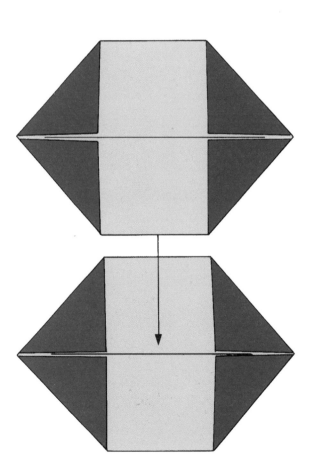

3. Repeat Steps 1 and 2 with second rectangle. Slide one rectangle halfway over the other.

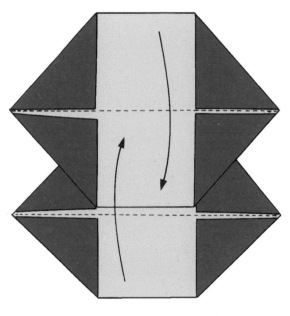

4. Fold up bottom flap and then fold down top flap.

5. Basic Unit. The two pockets on the top and bottom edges are used to combine units. If you don't have two pockets, make sure the flaps in Step 4 are folded one over the other.

Origami Furniture Pieces

These origami furniture pieces are perfect for doll houses and for making architectural settings. You can make different sized furniture by using larger or smaller pieces of paper. Be sure, however, to stick to the specified proportions. Construction paper is especially good for making these units.

CHAIR (Use four 6" x 4" rectangles)

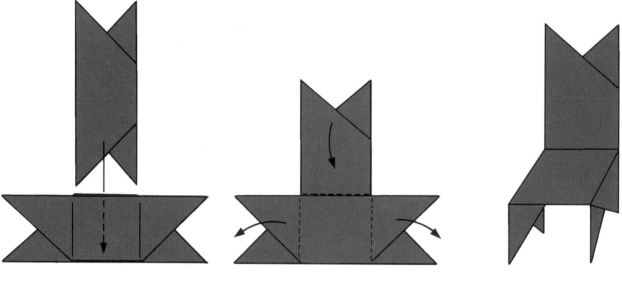

1. Fold two Basic Units. Slide one unit into pocket of other unit.

2. Fold down sides. Fold up back.

3. Chair.

SIDE TABLE OR FOOTSTOOL (Use two 6" x 4" rectangles)

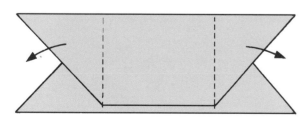

1. Fold a Basic Unit. Fold sides down.

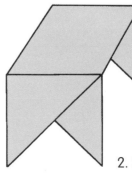

2. Side Table or Footstool.

Furniture Units 2
BENCH, SOFA, BED, DINING TABLE

BENCH (Use two 8" x 4" rectangles)

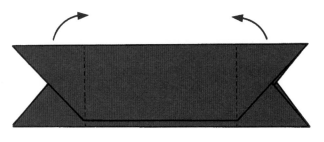

1. Fold a Basic Unit. Fold down sides.

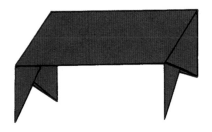

2. Bench.

SOFA (Use two 6" x 4" rectangles)

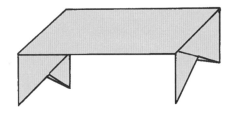

1. Use two rectangles to fold a Bench.

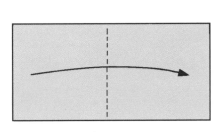

2. Fold third rectangle in half.

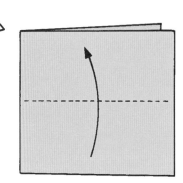

3. Fold in half again.

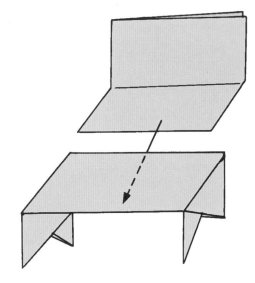

4. Slide into pocket of Bench.

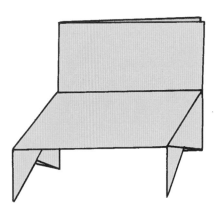

5. Sofa.

Creating New Models

You can create many different models by thinking of these Furniture Units as versatile building blocks. With a little imagination, you can make flowers, butterflies, jewelry, greeting cards, puzzles, and three-dimensional pictures by combining them in a variety of different ways.

BED (Use five 8" x 4" rectangles and one 6" x 4" rectangle)

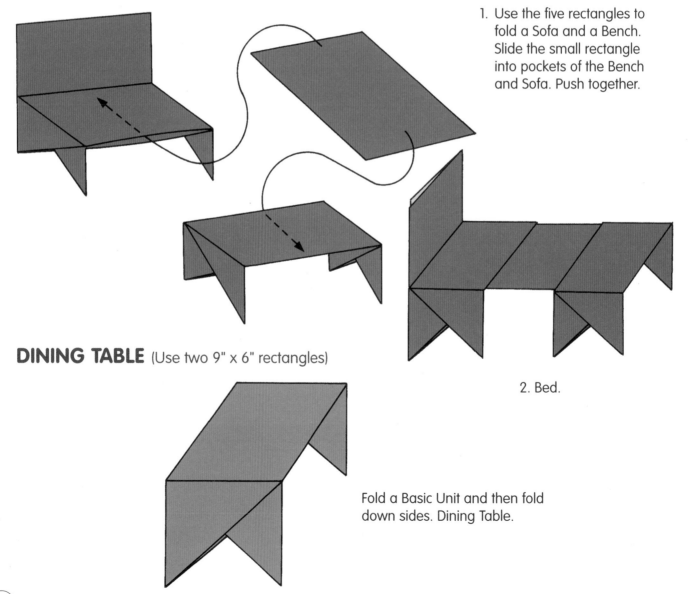

1. Use the five rectangles to fold a Sofa and a Bench. Slide the small rectangle into pockets of the Bench and Sofa. Push together.

2. Bed.

DINING TABLE (Use two 9" x 6" rectangles)

Fold a Basic Unit and then fold down sides. Dining Table.